GOATs IN SPORTS

BASKETBALL GOATs

KENNY ABDO

Fly!
An Imprint of Abdo Zoom
abdobooks.com

abdobooks.com

Published by Abdo Zoom, a division of ABDO, P.O. Box 398166, Minneapolis, Minnesota 55439. Copyright © 2025 by Abdo Consulting Group, Inc. International copyrights reserved in all countries. No part of this book may be reproduced in any form without written permission from the publisher. Fly!™ is a trademark and logo of Abdo Zoom.

Printed in the United States of America, North Mankato, Minnesota.
052024
092024

THIS BOOK CONTAINS RECYCLED MATERIALS

Photo Credits: Alamy, AP Images, Getty Images, Icon Sportswire, Shutterstock
Production Contributors: Kenny Abdo, Jennie Forsberg, Grace Hansen
Design Contributors: Candice Keimig, Neil Klinepier

Library of Congress Control Number: 2023948502

Publisher's Cataloging-in-Publication Data

Names: Abdo, Kenny, author.
Title: Basketball GOATs / by Kenny Abdo
Description: Minneapolis, Minnesota : Abdo Zoom, 2025 | Series: GOATs in sports | Includes online resources and index.
Identifiers: ISBN 9781098285647 (lib. bdg.) | ISBN 9781098286347 (ebook) | ISBN 9781098286699 (Read-to-me eBook)
Subjects: LCSH: Basketball--Juvenile literature. | Basketball teams--Juvenile literature. | Basketball—Records--United States--Juvenile literature. | Professional athletes--Juvenile literature.
Classification: DDC 796.323--dc23

TABLE OF CONTENTS

Basketball GOATs 4

The Greats 8

Scoreboard 20

Glossary 22

Online Resources 23

Index 24

BASKETBALL GOATs

In 1891, with a peach basket, a ball, and 13 simple rules, gym teacher James Naismith introduced his students to the game of "Basket Ball."

Little did Naismith know that his game would someday be known worldwide. It would also produce some of the greatest athletes, from George Mikan to LeBron James.

THE GREATS

Bill Russell won 11 **championships** with the Boston Celtics. With an **average** of 22.5 **rebounds** per game, he was one of the best defenders of his time. Russell received five **MVP** Awards.

Wilt Chamberlain set many records. One of his most impressive came in 1962. He scored 100 points in a single game for Philadelphia. Chamberlain held the points scored record with more than 31,000 points until a certain 7 foot 2 inch player came along.

Kareem Abdul-Jabbar was a tower of talent. He brought the Milwaukee Bucks their first **title** in 1971. Abdul-Jabbar joined the Los Angeles Lakers in 1975. There, he won five NBA **Finals**. Abdul-Jabbar also created the iconic "sky hook" shot!

Larry Bird ruled the court during the 1980s. He led the Celtics to three **titles**! Bird earned three straight regular season **MVP** Awards. He was also the NBA **Final** MVP twice.

Magic Johnson's playmaking and shooting skills helped lead the Lakers to winning five NBA **championships**. Magic was also honored with three NBA **Final MVP** Awards in the process.

Michael Jordan's unreal talent captured the world during the '90s. **Averaging** more than 30 points per game, Jordan led the Chicago Bulls to winning an incredible six NBA **championships**.

Shaquille O'Neal controlled the court with his size and power. Soaring 7 feet and 1 inch, he was an unstoppable force at center. Shaq sealed three **championships** with the Lakers and one with the Miami Heat.

Kobe Bryant had an incredible career with the Lakers. With his amazing scoring skills, Bryant hit more than 33,000 points. Bryant won five **championships** while inspiring countless fans.

LeBron James left a lasting mark on the NBA. James' ability to see the play and strong passing skills helped him secure four NBA **championships** and several records.

When it comes to three-pointers, Stephen Curry conquers the court. The four-time NBA **champion** has hit at least 10 threes per game more than 20 times. Curry was voted **MVP** twice.

The GOATs of basketball have **assisted** in taking their sport from a school gym to one of the most popular games in the world.

GLOSSARY

assist – supported or to have given aid; when a player made a pass that led directly to a basket.

average – a number found by adding the total rebounds or points scored in each game by the amount of games.

champion – the winner of a championship.

championship – a game held to find a first-place winner.

Finals – in the NBA, the annual championship series.

MVP – short for "most valuable player," an award given in sports to a player who has performed the best in a game or series.

rebound – the ball's bounce off the backboard or rim after a missed shot, or the act of catching the ball after its bounce.

title – a first-place position in a contest.

ONLINE RESOURCES

To learn more about the GOATs in Basketball, please visit **abdobooklinks.com** or scan this QR code. These links are routinely monitored and updated to provide the most current information available.

INDEX

Abdul-Jabbar, Kareem 11

Bird, Larry 12

Bryant, Kobe 16

Bucks 11

Celtics 9, 12

Chamberlain, Wilt 10

Curry, Stephen 18

James, LeBron 7, 17

Johnson, Earvin "Magic" 13

Jordan, Michael 14

Lakers 11, 15, 16

Mikan, George 7

Naismith, James 4, 7

O'Neal, Shaquille 15

Russell, Bill 9